Serious Chat A Kickass Guide to Spiritual Life

Eliot Highfield

Published by Eliot Highfield, 2024.

SERIOUS CHAT A KICKASS GUIDE TO SPIRITUAL LIFE

First edition. March 30, 2024.

Copyright © 2024 Eliot Highfield.

ISBN: 979-8224749171

Written by Eliot Highfield.

Table of Contents

Introduction: The Ultimate Soul Ride Awaits... You In?

Yo, soul-searcher. Ever found yourself under a moonlit sky, sipping on some age-old brew, mind swirling with the cosmic "Whys?" Nah, not pondering about the drink— but this wild, beautiful chaos we call life? That deep, nagging pulse, the questions that don't let you sleep?

Bingo. You've hit the universal jackpot. We all feel that pull. And that's where this gem comes in.

We're plunging straight into life's mind-benders. The big ones. The ones that had the best of us— poets, sages, your next-door neighbor— scratching heads and sometimes wiping away a sneaky tear. Puzzling over love's mad game? Trying to snatch a moment of zen amidst life's daily circus? We gotcha.

We'll zigzag through relationship mazes, tackle life's sucker punches, and, yes, even ponder on the big cosmic energy— be it God, the Universe, or just the vibe of the cosmos. And 'cause we're about that authentic life, expect tales from the heart, a healthy dose of chuckles (life's too short, right?), and wisdom from souls who've tread these paths before.

Trust us, it's an odyssey. Seasoned spirit-guru or just kickstarting your cosmic journey, there's gold here for you. Dive deep, laugh from your belly, let a tear or two drop, and unearth the magnificent universe within.

Feeling the pull? That's the call. Let's dive. Ready to unlock life? Let's roll.

Chapter 1: Understanding the Self

Hey there, curious soul! Ever felt like you're caught in a cosmic game of hide-and-seek with yourself? Like you're the detective of your own mystery novel, minus the dramatic rain-soaked alleys and fedoras? (Though hats could be fun, right?)

Buckle up, pal, 'cause we're diving deep. Ever wondered what's the deal with life and why that pizza last night felt like a spiritual experience?

From the brain-boggling "What's the meaning of life?" to the heartfelt "What's my vibe, and why's my soul jamming to it?", your burning questions are covered.

Picture this: Socrates, Buddha, and Shakespeare walk into a bar. After some rad philosophical debates and a karaoke session, they start dishing out the 411 on self-love, spirit, and why happiness sometimes feels like chasing a sneaky, tail-wagging puppy.

Ready to unlock the mysteries of your mind, soul, and that weird dream you had about flying tacos? You're in for a ride (and yeah, no gas money required). You might just end up high-fiving your reflection by the end.

Curiosity piqued? Good. Dive in, brave explorer. The cosmos ain't got nothing on the universe inside you. Adventure awaits!

What is the meaning of life?

Let's dive into that age-old question: What is the meaning of Life? Here's the scoop, served straight from the wisdom kitchen of some legendary folks:

1. Buddha: "Find Your Balance, Dude."

Life's a tightrope. Lean too much? You'll topple. Buddha's tip? Middle way. Less wobble, more groove. Oh, and maybe ditch those clunky shoes. Balance in style!

2. Jesus Christ: "Love. That's The Jam!"

Ever heard of JC's top track? It's all 'bout Love. Love your neighbor, your frenemy, even that guy who stole your parking spot. Spread the love vibes. And maybe share your playlist.

3. Muhammad: "Life? Journey to God."

Muhammad's take? We're all on this spiritual road trip. No GPS is needed, just faith. And hey, if you hit a pothole, that's just Life's way of saying, "Speed bump ahead!"

4. Confucius: "Be Good, Live Good."

Simple, right? For our man Confucius, it's all about character. You wanna level up in Life? Start with kindness. Bonus points if you laugh at bad dad jokes!

5. Socrates: "Know Thyself. No BS."

You know those soul-searching nights? Socrates was all about that. Dive deep. Get real with yourself. Ever tried to mirror pep talks? Game changer!

6. Rumi: "You're The Universe. No Kidding."

Rumi, that poetic genius, believed you're a universe. Cosmic, right? So next time you feel small, remember: you've got galaxies inside. Twinkle on!

7. Marcus Aurelius: "Life? It's In Your Head."

Old Marcus had a point. Life's what you make of it. Got lemons? Think lemonade, not sour faces. Mindset is your superpower. Use it!

Hey, superstar, these big brains had some wise takes, but guess what? Your Life, your rules. Grab that wisdom, sprinkle it in your favor, and make it legendary!

What is my purpose in life?

Let's crack that big ol' chestnut: What is my purpose in life? Buckle up, 'cause the wisdom train's chuggin' along, bringing insights from the cool kids of yesteryears:

1. Plato: "Reach for Your Best Self."

Plato was all, "Strive for the ideal." In non-philosopher talk? Be the best you. Maybe that's rockstar you. Or maybe chef-extraordinaire you. Hey, even cat-whisperer you. Go for gold!

2. Lao Tzu: "Flow, Don't Push."

Life's a river, dude. Lao Tzu? He says, "Go with the flow." So, paddle less, float more. Oh, and if you spot a waterfall? Epic selfie moment!

3. Aristotle: "Find Your Groove. Do Good."

Ari broke it down. It's all about your 'thing.' That thing that fires you up and, bonus, helps others. Maybe it's knitting. Or karaoke. Find it. Rock it. Spread the joy!

4. da Vinci: "Stay Curious, Pal."

Leonardo was the OG-curious cat. Paint, invent, scribble. His mantra? Keep exploring. So next time you think, "Why?" Go one better and try, "Why not?"

5. Galileo: "Question Everything. Yep, Everything."

Galileo was that kid in class, "But why?" Be more Galileo. Peek under life's rug. Question, learn, grow. Oh, and maybe don't peek under your actual rug. Dust bunnies. Eek!

6. Rumi: "Listen to Your Heart. It Knows."

Rumi's take? Your heart's a compass. Feeling lost? Tune in. It's got directions, feelings, and probably a playlist of soulful beats. Heart FM, anyone?

7. Marcus Aurelius: "Reflect. Act. Repeat."

Marcus dropped this wisdom nugget: Life's a loop. Think, act, reflect. Got a dream? Chase it. Mess up? It's cool. Reflect, rinse, repeat. Just remember to hydrate!

Alright, brave soul, history's VIPs have dropped their two cents. Now, over to you. Remember, your life's story is yours to write. Pen in hand, dream in heart, let's make it epic!

What is the soul?

Ah, the big "soul" question! It was time to put on our wisdom caps and see what the legends had to say. Ready for a trip down enlightenment lane?

1. Buddha: "It's Complex, Buddy."

Buddha would be like, "Soul? It ain't static." Think of it like your Netflix list. Ever-changing. Sometimes deep, sometimes... just in the mood for a rom-com. Go figure!

2. Jesus: "Eternal Spark Inside."

JC put it simply: It's God's breath in you. It's that little light, even when life's a blackout. And remember, even on bad hair days, your Soul's still shining bright.

3. Muhammad: "God's Essence, Yo."

For Muhammad, the Soul's divine stuff. You're a bit of the cosmic pie! And while pies are tasty, souls? Infinitely cooler.

4. Socrates: "Your Inner Pilot."

Soc was all about the inner voice. That nag telling you, "Don't text your ex." or "Yeah, maybe not that 3rd donut." Listen up, it's got your back!

5. Confucius: "Moral Compass in Action."

Good ol' Confucius believed the Soul guided your deeds. Like your moral GPS. Did you miss a turn? Just recalibrate. And maybe grab some snacks for the ride.

6. Rumi: "Universe Dancing Inside."

Our man Rumi was poetic AF. For him, the Soul was love, ecstasy, and a wild dance. So, next time you dance in your PJs? That's just the universe getting its groove on.

7. Plato: "Eternal and Immortal Dude!"

Plato's vibe? Your Soul's old, like ancient. It's been around, seen stuff, got the T-shirt. So, while your body's all about 2023, your Soul? Timeless rockstar.

Hey, champ! The Soul's one deep rabbit hole. Everyone's got their take, and guess what? Your personal feel on it matters most. So, while you ponder, remember: soul-searching is soul-searching's more than just a catchy phrase. Dive deep, dance wild, and let your Soul lead the way!

What is self-love?

Buckle up, superstar; we're diving into the juicy world of self-love! And trust me, this ain't just about bubble baths and chocolates (though, yum!). Let's break it down with wisdom from the bigwigs of history:

1. Buddha: "Kindness Begins at Home."

Buddy Buddha would say, "Treat yourself like you'd treat your BFF." Making mistakes? It's cool. A learning curve, bro! Could you go easy on ya?

2. Jesus: "Neighbor = You."

JC once said, "Love thy neighbor as thyself." So, if you're down for loving your neighbor, don't forget the 'as yourself' part. Wink, wink.

3. Confucius: "Inner Respect, Dude."

Confucius was all about respecting yourself. Not in a braggy way, but knowing your worth. So, wear that invisible crown. And maybe a cape. Capes rock.

4. Rumi: "You're the Universe."

To Rumi, you're the whole universe in ecstatic motion. Basically, you're a cosmic party. Pop the confetti!

5. Aristotle: "Know Thyself."

Good ol' Ari was like, "Know yourself, love yourself." So, date night with yourself? It's totally a thing. Pizza is optional. But not really.

6. Lao Tzu: "Be Your Own Rock."

Lao Tzu would say, "You're your own mountain." Solid, majestic, a bit rocky. But hey, those views? Totally worth the climb.

7. Marcus Aurelius: "Inner Fortress FTW!"

Big M believed in being your own fortress. Rough day? Retreat inside, chill with your thoughts, and come out stronger. Like a mental superhero cape!

Hey, rockstar! Self-love ain't just a buzzword; it's a lifestyle. It's the cozy blanket on life's couch. So snuggle in, grab your wisdom book, and remember: You're the main character in your story. Be your own biggest fan!

How to be happy with yourself?

1. Buddha's Take: Inner peace isn't a myth; it's your birthright. You've been looking far and wide, but have you tried peeping in the mirror? It may be time for a chat with yourself. Settle in, breathe deep, and check-in. Remember, meditation doesn't require a mountaintop, sometimes just a comfy couch.

2. Jesus' Nudge: Loving others? Noble! But first, how about some self-love? Embrace those imperfections; they're the stitches in your unique tapestry. The way your eyes crinkle when you laugh, the irregular rhythm of your heart; these are miracles. Celebrate them.

3. Rumi's Whisper: Listen closely. You're not just a speck; you're the universe expressing itself. Deep, right? So next time you feel small, remember you're made of star stuff. Dance like the whole galaxy is cheering for you. Because, in a way, it is.

4. Einstein's Flash: You've got energy, potential, and, dare we say, genius inside. Don't believe it? If energy is constant (thanks, Albert!), you've always got more to give. Even on those bed-head days, remind yourself: "This is just my 'relativity' look!"

5. Plato's Quickie: Dive deep into the ocean of self-knowledge. Yep, it might get a bit stormy, but the treasures you'll find? Priceless. When did you last sit down, minus distractions, and ask yourself the big questions? And by big, we mean, "If I was a pizza topping, which one would I be?"

6. Shakespeare's Wink: All the world's your stage. Sure, there's drama, tears, and occasional stage fright. But the applause, the victories? Oh, they're worth the script! Own your role. And when in doubt, remember: There's no shame in rehearsing in your jammies.

7. Dalai Lama's Zen Tip: True joy comes from within. But hey, a killer playlist doesn't hurt. Start your morning with a smile, end

your evening with gratitude. Caught yourself daydreaming and chuckling? Perfect, you're on the right track. Life's got its ups and downs, but with a touch of inner joy, it's a wild, worthy ride.

What is the relationship between mind, body, and spirit?

Oh, snap! We're diving deep into the cosmic trinity: mind, body, and spirit. Let's see how our OG philosophers and spiritual heavyweights break it down:

1. Buddha: "It's All Connected, Pal."

For Buddha, the mind, body, and spirit are like a trio band. Mind's on vocals, body's jamming on the guitar, and spirit's drumming away. Balance is key. And no solo acts!

2. Jesus: "Unity, My Dude."

JC emphasized harmony. The mind thinks, the body acts, and the spirit loves. It's like a divine relay race. The baton? Pure love. Run with it.

3. Aristotle: "Three's a Party!"

Ari said the soul animates the body, and reason (mind) is our jam. So, the body's dancing, the mind's choosing the tunes, and the spirit's bringing the vibes.

4. Rumi: "Mind Dreams, Body Dances, Spirit Loves."

Rumi-style? Mind's the dreamer; the body's the dancer; the spirit's the love. So, boogie with passion. And maybe wear comfy shoes!

5. Confucius: "Harmony Rocks!"

For Confucius, it's about alignment. Mindsets the goal, body hustles, spirit keeps it real. Teamwork makes the dream work, right?

6. Lao Tzu: "Flow, Baby, Flow."

Lao Tzu was all about Tao – the flow. Mind's the plan; body's the action; spirit's the flow. Go with it, and remember: paddles are optional!

7. Plato: "Chariot Vibes!"

Plato had this chariot analogy. Mind's the charioteer, body, and spirit are the horses. Reign them in, or it's off-road adventures for you. And maybe pack snacks?

Alrighty, rockstar! Mind, body, and spirit are life's ultimate trio. It's like your internal GPS, workout buddy, and pep squad all rolled into one. Tune in, sync up, and let the magic happen. And hey, if they ever drop an album? Bet it'd be a cosmic hit!

How can I deepen my spiritual connection?

Alright, buddy, want to crank up that spiritual volume? Here's some wisdom, sprinkled with a little' humor, from the greats to get you vibing higher:

1. Buddha's Chill Suggestion: "Meditate. It's like a spa day for your soul. And who doesn't love a good spa day? Gives that inner voice a microphone."
2. Jesus' Beach Walk Talk: "Pray. It's like sending a DM straight to the Big Guy. No WiFi is needed. Just pure, heart-to-heart connection."
3. Rumi's Campfire Poetry: "Love more. It's the universe's music. Dance to it! Even if you've got two left feet."
4. Gandhi's Peaceful Protest: "Serve others. It's like a BOGO deal – helps them elevate you. That's spiritual multitasking!"
5. Marcus Aurelius' Diary Entry: "Reflect daily. Journal or just ponder. Dive deep. No snorkels allowed."
6. Lao Tzu's Nature Walk: "Flow like water. Adapt, change, grow. And hey, stay hydrated while you're at it."
7. Dalai Lama's Coffee Shop Wisdom: "Be kind. Kindness is the universal language. Even if you're bad at accents."

Want to go deeper? Dive in. Your spiritual journey is like an all-you-can-eat buffet – keep going back until you're full..

How can I live with authenticity?

Hey, looking to keep it 100% real? Here are some gold nuggets of wisdom from our wise-guy crew, with a pinch of sass for taste:

1. Socrates' Street Talk: "Know thyself. It's the OG self-help tip. Check yourself before you wreck yourself."
2. Shakespeare's Theatre Whisper: "Be true to you. Everyone else's part is taken anyway. So, no understudies needed."
3. Buddha's Chill Tip: "Ditch the mask. Being two-faced is such a last lifetime. Plus, it's bad for the skin."
4. Friedrich Nietzsche's Bar Advice: "Embrace your passions. Life ain't a rehearsal. It's the main gig!"
5. Rumi's Night Sky Gazing: "Listen to your heart. It's got the beats. And not just on Spotify."
6. Maya Angelou's Coffee Shop Musings: "Your story matters. Own it. It's the best book you'll ever write."
7. Da Vinci's Art Class: "Express yourself. Paint, dance, sing. Even if your dog's the only fan."

Wanna live authentically? Remember, it's less about perfection and more about direction. And occasionally, ordering the extra fries because, hey, that's you!

How can I overcome my spiritual challenges?

Ready to kick those spiritual bumps to the curb? Let's pull some wisdom from the Hall of Famers and mix in a dash of street flair:

1. **Buddha's Extended Beach Vibes:** Ever watched the waves hit the shore, retreat, and come back again? That's like our attachments. We get so caught up holding onto things. Imagine grasping wet sand; it slips through. Buddha's telling us, "Hold it gently, dude. Enjoy it while it lasts, but don't lose your cool when it's gone." Life's a beach; enjoy the waves without getting sunburnt.

2. **Jesus' Extended Campfire Tales:** So, you're sitting around a campfire, roasting marshmallows, and that one cousin brings up old beef. Frustrating, right? But Jesus was like, "Forgive, not for them, but for you." When you forgive, you're not just letting them off the hook; you're freeing yourself from carrying that heavy grudge backpack.

3. **Lao Tzu's Extended Traffic Tip:** Ever been stuck in traffic, honking, frustrated because you can't speed up? Lao Tzu's wisdom is like that chill passenger saying, "Relax, we'll get there." Instead of pushing against what's natural, sometimes you just gotta cruise, go with the flow, and jam to some tunes. Life ain't a race; it's a road trip.

4. **Rumi's Extended Dance Club Beats:** Rumi was like that buddy who drags you to the dance floor when you're not feeling it. Pain, heartbreak, Monday blues? Feel it, accept it, then shake it off. Even if you've got two left feet, dance like nobody's watching. It's therapy, only with better music.

5. **Dalai Lama's Extended Coffee Chat:** Picture sipping coffee with the Dalai Lama. He leans in and says, "Compassion's the

real magic brew." It ain't about the caffeine kick but the warmth you spread. Show kindness; it's like an espresso shot for the soul.

6. **Averroes' Telescope Insight:** Averroes would probably be that friend who drags you to a midnight stargazing trip. As you gaze at the vastness, he'd whisper, "Always seek knowledge." Just like the endless stars, there's always more to learn. Don't just scratch the surface; dive into the cosmic ocean of knowledge.

7. **Gandhi's Farmers' Market Wisdom:** Imagine shopping with Gandhi at a farmers' market. Between picking tomatoes and haggling prices, he'd drop, "Wanna change the world? Start with you." Choose goodness, kindness, and maybe some fresh produce. Small actions, big ripples.

Navigating spiritual challenges is like hiking. Rocky paths steep climbs, but oh, those views! Keep pushing, breathe, and always pack some wisdom snacks!.

Chapter 2: Emotions and Inner Peace

Alright, legends of the now, hold onto your hearts and feels! Chapter 2 is about to unveil a transformative odyssey - "Emotions and Inner Peace." Buckle in; this ain't your grandma's self-help.

Joyful Journeys: Ever felt there's gotta be more to life than this? Dive deep! We're unlocking happiness so radiant even Buddha would need shades!

Pursue the Peace: Think peace is a pipedream? Think again! Let's reveal the serene trails once roamed by Jesus and Lao Tzu. You in?

Present Moment Mastery: Are you tired of your mind playing time-travel tricks? Einstein vibes ahead! We're about to anchor you right here, right now.

Grief's Grace: Bearing a heartache that feels endless? Lean in. Together, we'll unveil healing as timeless as Rumi's verses.

Face Your Fears: The unknown's got nothing on you. Armed with Galileo's courage, we'll turn those mountains of dread into molehills.

Heartfelt Huddle: Ready to supercharge your empathy? Dive into a realm where hearts aren't just worn on sleeves but blaze like stars!

Acceptance Allure: Life's a dance. Epictetus knew. Join us to groove with grace, embracing every high and low.

Gratitude Galore: Ready to be drenched in thankfulness? Dive into the fountain of life's greatest gift.

Hear that? It's your soul yearning for this transformative journey. Dive in, rise, and let's resonate together. Passionate as a sun's core, persuasive as the moon's pull – this chapter is your gateway to emotional euphoria! Dive in.

How to be happy?

Alright, buddy, let's dive deep and unearth the golden ticket to Happyville, taking wisdom from the big shots of yesteryears:

1. Buddha's Chill Pill: "Craving less, living more." Life's not about grabbing everything. Feel the moment, and let go of that FOMO. Simplicity's underrated!
2. Jesus' Gem: "Give and vibe." Generosity, mate. It's the secret sauce. Help a neighbor, or share those fries. Your heart? It'll do the cha-cha.
3. Socrates Says: "Know yourself, pal." Dive into that noggin of yours. The more you get you, the less those blues stick around.
4. Confucius Confesses: "Balance, baby!" Not just for tightrope walkers. Get your hustle and rest in sync. And maybe don't binge-watch cat videos till 3 AM.
5. Rumi's Riddle: "Seek joy within." External goodies? Fleeting. But that inner glow? Stickier than bubblegum on a summer sidewalk.
6. Einstein's Equation: "Curiosity = dope days." Explore. Wonder. Ask why your cat's obsessed with that laser pointer. Life's richer when you're digging it.
7. Gandhi's Groove: "Be the change." Feeling meh? Pivot. Lighten your load, and maybe the world's, one tiny good vibe at a time.

Roll with these, and watch happiness do the boogie in your life. You got this!

How to find peace?

Alright, amigo, need a peace piece? Let's surf on wisdom waves from some legendary peeps and snag that tranquility treasure:

1. **Buddha's Buzz:** "Be here. Now." Don't let your brain time-travel. Past's dusty, future's foggy. Enjoy this very breath. And maybe this donut. Yum.
2. **Lao Tzu's Logic:** "Flow, don't force." Like water, mate. Glide through the tough spots. Don't be that square peg in a round hole. Ouch.
3. **Jesus' Jam:** "Forgive and float." Grudges? They're like carrying a cactus. Set it down. Walk away. No more prickly problems.
4. **Marcus Aurelius' Memo:** "Control the controllable." Can't change the rain, but you can rock that umbrella. Look snazzy, stay dry.
5. **Rumi's Recipe:** "Seek inside, not outside." Got a void? Can't Amazon Prime fulfillment. It's an inside job. Meditation, maybe?
6. **Shakespeare's Shimmer:** "All's well that ends well." Rough patches? Temporary. Remember, after a drama, there's always a curtain call and applause.
7. **Einstein's Insight:** "Embrace wonder." Ponder the stars. Or why does toast always fall jam-side down? Amazement? It's a stress-buster.

Ride these vibes, and you'll be coasting to Peaceville in no time. Keep it groovy!

How to live in the present moment?

Alright, buddy, wanna drop that time-travel habit and groove in the here and now? Here's the 411 from some OG thinkers and modern homies:

1. Buddha's Beat: "Breath's where it's at." Inhale. Exhale. Repeat. Feelin' those air vibes? You're doing it. Simplicity's slick, huh?
2. Lao Tzu's Tip: "Ditch the baggage." Yesterday's gone. Tomorrow's a mystery ticket. Today? It's your main event. Live it up!
3. Epictetus' Echo: ✕ "Circle of control, dude." If you can't change it, don't sweat it. Energy is precious. Don't waste it on reruns.
4. Rumi's Riff: "Feel, don't think." Emotions are the music of the soul. Dance with 'em. In the rain. Or your kitchen. No judgment.
5. Mother Teresa's Tidbit: "Love the one in front." Give your full focus to whoever's with ya. Be all ears. And maybe a shoulder.
6. Shakespeare's Share: "Play your part now." Life's a stage. This moment's your scene. Don't miss your cue. Steal the show!
7. Einstein's Equation: "Time's relative." The present is a gift. That's why it's called "present". Get it? Unwrap it. Enjoy.

Remember, the now's where the magic's at. No rewinds or fast-forwards. Just play. And slay.

How to deal with grief and loss?

Dude, life can toss some real curveballs. Grief's tough, no lie. If you're ridin' that emotional roller coaster, here's the lowdown from some wise cats:

1. Buddha's Vibe: "Change's the only constant." Pain's proof you've loved hard. Embrace the feels, even the messy ones. It's part of healing.
2. Rumi's Real Talk: "The wound is where the light enters." Pain's a teacher. Let it guide, not destroy. You'll shine brighter. Promise.
3. Confucius' Cool Tip: "Growth from grief." Every tear's like water to a seed. Grow stronger. And taller. Branch out!
4. Mother Teresa's Take: "Lean on your crew." You ain't alone. Share. Care. Bear hugs help—a lot.
5. MLK Jr.'s Wisdom: "Keep moving forward." Step by step. At your own beat. No rush.
6. Aristotle's Angle: "Darkness brings stars." Loss illuminates what's precious. Cherish memories. They're your forever.
7. Freud's Fix: "Talk it out." Unpack those feelings. With a buddy, shrink, or your dog. Lettin' it out's half the battle.

Big hugs, mate. The sun always rises, even after the darkest nights. And hey, we're all in this crazy ride together. You got this.

How to cultivate compassion and empathy?

Hey, champ! Looking to add a dash more heart and soul into your life? Cool beans! Let's deep-dive with some timeless advice from the OG thinkers:

1. Dalai Lama's Dose: "Same boat, different seats." Realize everyone's fighting some battle. It just gets easier when you're kind.
2. Jesus' Jam: "Treat peeps like you wanna be treated." The golden rule, baby! Works every time.
3. Buddha's Beat: "Hearts wide open." Suffering is universal. Embrace it. Sharing the load makes it lighter, bro.
4. Rumi's Riff: "Love's the bridge." Differences? Meh. Focus on shared humanity. Love big, love often.
5. Confucius' Chirp: "Listen up!" Give folks your full attention. Makes them feel valued. It's magic!
6. Marcus Aurelius' Musing: "Walk in their shoes." Get their perspective. Imagine their journey. Insights? Priceless.
7. Mother Teresa's Tip: "See with heart-eyes." Beyond flaws and quirks. Deep dive into souls. There are real treasures there.

Dude, by flexing that compassion muscle, you're on the VIP list for a richer life. And remember, the world could always use more kind-hearted heroes. So, rock it!

How to practice radical acceptance?

Alright, rockstar, strap in! If you're craving some radical acceptance mojo, you're in luck. From the minds of some total legends, here's your playbook:

1. Buddha's Wisdom Bite: "Life's a ride!" It's got its ups and downs. Lean into it. The twists? They're just pit stops. Breathe. Accept. Move.
2. Aristotle's Two Cents: "Embrace the now!" Yesterday's gone. Tomorrow's a mystery. Dance in today's rain. Why fight the weather?
3. Rumi's Recipe: "Life ain't perfect." Expecting it? Haha, the joke's on you! Roll with the punches. Turn 'em into stories!
4. Lao Tzu's Truth Bomb: "Be water, my friend." Flow with life. Don't resist. Can't control the river's path? Paddle stronger.
5. Mother Teresa's Tidbit: "See the good." Is stuff messed up? Look again. Hidden blessings everywhere. Find 'em. Cherish 'em.
6. Marcus Aurelius' Mumble: "Universe has a plan." It's wild, right? Trust it. Things fit together, eventually. Even those wonky puzzle pieces.
7. Shakespeare's Shout: "All the world's a stage." Play your part. Embrace the script even when life throws tomatoes. Duck and laugh!

So, dive in, dude. Life's a trip and acceptance? It's your trusty compass. Navigate like a pro!

How to live in gratitude?

Superstar, wanna vibe on gratitude? Let's take a journey with the wisdom from some real OGs and sprinkle in a bit of that modern-day sauce:

1. Buddha's Gratitude Glimpse: "Savor small joys." That coffee? A miracle in a cup. Sun on your face? Nature's warm hug. Feel it. Dig it.
2. Jesus' Jam: "Blessings in disguise." Tough times? Look deeper. Silver linings, baby! They're hidden, but they're there. Seek and find.
3. Lao Tzu's Truth Tease: "Stay humble, stay grateful." You're a speck in the cosmos. But, dang, ain't it grand? Marvel at it all.
4. Rumi's Riff: "Love is always the answer." Got issues? Send love. Annoying neighbor? Love 'em. It's magic, trust me!
5. Epictetus' Epic Echo: "Desire what you have." Yearning for the new? Eh, overrated. Your old sneakers? Gold. Walk in gratitude.
6. Shakespeare's Share: "Life's a play, and you've got the best seat!" Applaud the highs. Respect the lows. Give a standing O to the universe.
7. Galileo's Gaze: "Stars above, wonders below." The night sky? Infinite wonders. Your life? Same, pal. Be starstruck by the everyday.

So, grab life by the gratitude, champ. It ain't just an attitude; it's a whole vibe!

Chapter 3: Relationships and Connections

Ahoy there, reader! Ready to dive into the deep, sometimes choppy, but always intriguing waters of human connections? We've all been there: pondering what love is while scarfing down ice cream or questioning why Aunt Carol seems to have a direct line to the Big Guy upstairs. Whether you're single and loving it, hitched and navigating coupledom, or just trying to find your place in the universe, this chapter is your trusty compass. We're decoding the love for the Man Upstairs, breaking down the feelings for our fellow humans, and getting honest about trusting the cosmos. So, pull up your cozy chair because we're diving deep into the heart's mysteries, laughing at life's quirks, and finding answers to questions like "Why the heck is love so complicated?". Let's unravel this tangled web of relationships and connections, shall we?

What Is Love?

1. Soul's Dance: Buddha once hinted love's like a cosmic dance. Souls are tangling, just vibing together. Think of a silent night with a full moon and your heart syncing with nature. Real deep.
2. Ultimate Gift: Taking a page from Jesus, love's all about giving without expecting, like giving away your last donut. It's hard hurts sometimes, but man, it's genuine and pure.
3. Rumi's Universe: Ah, Rumi! For him, love was intoxication, like being drunk without a drop of wine. It's that heady feeling when your heart seems to beat outside your chest. Crazy but true!
4. Einstein's Wonder: Love's kinda...relative? It's the energy driving the universe, man. Neither created nor destroyed. Just transforming, evolving. Heart meets science!
5. Lao Tzu's Wisdom: Imagine love as water. Ever flowing, adapting, nourishing. It's soft yet unstoppable. Love's power is in its gentleness. It's deep, man, deep.
6. Shakespeare's Stage: Billy Shakes viewed love as a play. Comedy, tragedy, a bit of drama. Sometimes you're the lead, sometimes just watching from the stalls. It's unpredictable!
7. Freud's Couch Trip: Delve deep, dude! Unpack those emotions. Love is a mix of past memories, dreams, and even unconscious desires. Sometimes twisted, but always fascinating. Dive into your mind!

Whew! Strap in, mate. Love's a rollercoaster. These hints? Just the start. Dive deeper and feel everything. Welcome to the heart's wild journey!

How to be happy in a relationship?

How to be happy in a relationship?

1. **Listen More, Talk Less:** Socrates once said, "Speak so I may see you." But in love, it's about listening. Hear 'em out, for real.
2. **Compromise:** As Buddha might say, the middle path is key. Not too much, not too little. Find balance together.
3. **Keep the Spark Alive:** Take notes from Shakespeare: Write a sonnet or heck, just send a flirty text. Romance isn't dead.
4. **Trust:** Galileo got heat for his beliefs. But in love? Trust is the sun. Don't let doubts cloud it.
5. **Learn Together:** Einstein said, "Life's a classroom." Explore, learn, and grow—together.
6. **Apologize (and mean it):** As Rumi hinted, mistakes are the entrance to truth. Say sorry, mean it, and move on.
7. **Self-Care:** Jesus Christ preached love for all. But don't forget you. Love yourself, then spread that joy.

Remember, love ain't a sprint; it's a marathon. And sometimes, you just need to tie those shoes tighter and keep running side by side.

1.

• How to be a happy single?

• Embrace Freedom: Confucius might say, "Embrace the road alone." No curfews, no check-ins. Just you. Pretty dope, right?

• Self-Discovery: Da Vinci was into self-portraits. Dive deep, pal. What's your Mona Lisa? Rediscover you.

• Friends & Fam Time: As old Aristotle hinted, "Quality > quantity." Few pals, more memories. Game night?

• Treat Yo' Self: Ever heard Buddha chat about inner peace? Spa day? Chocolate binge? Go wild. It's 'me time'.

• Goals & Grind: Like Einstein's $E=mc^2$, you're the energy. Crush those goals. New hobby? Heck, why not?

• Solo Adventures: Rumi says, "Explore the world within." But hey, the outer world's cool too. Road trip, anyone?

• Know You're Enough: Jesus, Gandhi, MLK—they believed in self-worth. Rock on, solo. You're the full package.

Remember, bud: solo ain't solo when you're your best company. Turn up the jams, dance like nobody's watching (because they ain't), and toast to the fabulous single you. Cheers!

What is love for God?

Alright, diving deep into the cosmic feels. Here's the 411:

1. Eternal Connection: Think of it like Wi-Fi. We're talking about the strongest signal to the main source. Always connected. No drop-offs.
2. Beyond Conditions: Jesus was all, "Love thy neighbor." But loving God? It's like loving your dog times infinity. No matter how messy life gets.
3. Ultimate Trust: Remember when Buddha mentioned letting go? Loving God is like handing over the steering wheel. Not knowing where you're headed, but knowing it's somewhere good.
4. Everyday Gratitude: Noticed that sunset? Or that random act of kindness? Little cosmic winks from above. Thanks, big G!
5. Devotion in Action: As Mother Teresa said, "Small things with great love." Every good deed, every smile, it's like sending a cosmic text: "Hey, thinking of you."
6. Seeking the Divine: It's that constant thirst. Like being at a concert, pushing to the front. Always trying to get a bit closer to the stage.
7. Feeling Seen: Ever felt alone in a crowd? With God's love, it's like having someone lock eyes with you from across the room. Seen and known, man.

In essence, love for God? It's the universe's most epic love story, with you as the lead. And the best part? The soundtrack slaps.

What is love for others?

Alright, pal, buckle up. We're diving deep into the whirlpool of feels—talkin' 'bout love for others. Ever scratched your head, wondering, "What's the deal?" Let me break it down with some wisdom nuggets.

1. Understanding is Key: Buddha might say, "To understand someone is to love them." Take time. Listen. Put yourself in their shoes. It's the real magic trick to deep love.
2. Eyes on the Soul: Jesus, while breaking bread, might've hinted, "Look beyond the face. The real deal? It's the soul." Loving someone ain't about looks; it's about feeling that heart connect.
3. Let Love Breathe: Lao Tzu, while watching clouds, could've advised, "Love ain't a caged bird. Let it fly, let it return." Trust is the air love breathes.
4. Embrace the Flaws: Shakespeare, between sonnets, might've chuckled, "Love's about embracing quirks." So she snores? Or he can't dance? That's the loveable bit!
5. Growth Together: Aristotle, with scrolls scattered, would likely note, "Two souls, growing as one, that's the golden ticket." Evolve, change, grow – but do it together.
6. Stay Present: Mother Teresa, among the needy, might've whispered, "Love is now. This moment." Forget the past; don't stress the future—love in the present.
7. Deep Dive: Rumi, under starlit skies, probably penned, "Dive deep into love's ocean. That's where treasures are." Surface level isn't enough. Dive deep into understanding, patience, and trust.

Remember, buddy, I love's that old vinyl record. It might have scratches and skips, but the music? Pure gold. Dive in, dance like no one's watching, and let that soul shine. Ain't nothing quite like it.

How to trust in the universe?

Have you ever felt like the world's spinning madly, and you're just trying to find your groove? Like looking for your phone in a messy room, sometimes you gotta trust that it's there, even if you can't see it. So, let's chat trusting the universe, the way folks who've been around the wisdom block might've said it but jazzed up for us regular Joes:

1. Go With the Flow: Lao Tzu, chillin' by a river, might've said, "Water flows, not fights." Don't push against Life's current. Sometimes, it's just about riding the wave.
2. It's All Connected: Picture Einstein, wild hair and all chuckling, "Everything's relative, pal!" Every choice, every twist, every dang turn – it's all weaving your unique tapestry.
3. Let Go and Let Be: Buddha, under his tree, would probably advise, "Attachment? That's a pain-bringer." Release that death grip on outcomes. Breathe. Release. Trust.
4. Embrace Uncertainty: Shakespeare, scribbling away, might've quipped, "Life's a play, and we're off-script!" Surprises ain't always bad. Sometimes, they're standing ovations in disguise.
5. Life's Got Rhythms: Think of Rumi, dancing in the moonlight, whispering, "Life's got beats. Highs. Lows. It's all part of the dance." Trust the rhythm, even if you miss a step or two.
6. Nature Knows: Mother Teresa, feeling a breeze, might've murmured, "Nature doesn't hurry, yet all's accomplished." Trees don't stress about growing. They just do.
7. Stay Open: Marcus Aurelius, in between ruling Rome, might've noted, "The universe ain't out to get you. It's here with lessons." Good, bad, ugly – it's all teaching you something.

And hey, when in doubt, just remember: The universe has been around for a hot minute. It's seen stars born and fade, and it's still spinning. So, chin up, trust the process, and believe you're right where you should be. You got this!

Chapter 4: Facing Challenges and Growing

Ever felt like life's got a personal vendetta against you? Like, why's it gotta be so hard? Well, here's the secret: It ain't just you. Dive into this chapter, and you'll discover:

- Ways to bounce back when life throws its worst curveballs.

- How forgiving someone can be the ultimate power move.

- Letting go of the stuff dragging you down? We got the how-to.

- Unpacking the mysteries: Why the heck does suffering even exist?

- Hunting down those rays of hope in a world that sometimes feels downright gloomy.

- Harnessing your inner badass when fear's knocking on your door.

- The art of giving up control without losing yourself.

Peek behind the curtain of life's toughest questions, guided by the words of some legendary wise folks, all while speaking your language. Got your attention? Good, let's dive in and get real.

Courage ain't about not feeling fear. It's about grabbing fear by the collar and saying, "You're riding shotgun, pal!" Keep flexing those courage muscles, champ. The world's got nothing on you!

How to overcome adversity?

Yo, ever been smacked upside the head by life and thought, "Why me?" We've all been there. But here's the deal: adversity's like that annoying neighbor – it's going nowhere. So, what's the trick to dance in the rain instead of just getting wet? Let's break it down:

1. Breathe, Bro! - Buddha once said, "Pain is certain; suffering is optional." In plain English? Sh*t happens. But sulking? Nah. When life throws punches and deep breaths. In, out. Ride the wave.
2. Flex that Faith - JC (yeah, Jesus) was all about turning the other cheek. But not like, "let life slap you around." More like, trust the process. You got this, champ!
3. Grind and Shine - Remember Confucius? Dude said, "Our greatest glory ain't in never falling, but rising every time." Dust off. Rise up. Repeat.
4. Change the Channel - Socrates mused, "The secret of change is to focus energy on building the new." Got problems? Sure. But focus on solutions, pal.
5. Hug it Out - Rumi whispered, "The wound is where the light enters." Sounds trippy, right? But think: every scar's a story. Own it. Grow from it. And maybe, get a tattoo?
6. One Step at a Time - Our boy Einstein said, "Life's like riding a bicycle. To keep balance, ya gotta keep moving." Rough patches? Yep. But move forward. One foot. Then the next.
7. Laugh a Little - Shakespeare, the OG wordsmith, hinted, "With mirth and laughter let old wrinkles come." So when life's a drag, chuckle. It confuses your problems.

There ya have it. Overcoming adversity ain't about dodging raindrops but learning to groove in the storm. Hold on tight, and remember: after the darkest nights come the brightest dawns. Let's ride this rollercoaster called life together, alright? Keep that chin up!

How to forgive?

Yo, ever felt like a boiling teapot because someone did ya dirty? It's rough, I get it. But holding onto that heat? Not good for your soul-coffee, my friend. Let's spill the tea on this forgiveness thing:

1. Feel it First - Our boy Buddha said, "Holding onto anger is like drinking poison." So, feel mad, sad, rad. But don't chug that poison. Let it out, shout it out.
2. It's for You, Boo - JC (that's Jesus Christ) was like, "Forgive others, and you'll be forgiven." But here's the deal: it's more for you than them. Cleanse that heart.
3. Rewrite that Story - Confucius dropped, "He who seeks revenge should dig two graves." Translation: revenge ain't the way. Flip the script. You're the author.
4. Wipe that Slate - Remember Plato? The dude said, "Wise men speak because they have something to say." So chat it out, let it out, and find closure. No ghosting.
5. Embrace the Ouch - Rumi, all mysterious-like, whispered, "The cure for pain is in the pain." Sounds whack, right? But facing the hurt? That's where healing's at.
6. Growth Game Strong - Einstein's vibe was, "Life is like riding a bike." So when you skid, remember scars show growth. Learn. Live. Forgive.
7. Set Free the Bee - Shakespeare said, "Forgiveness is the fragrance the violet sheds on the heel that crushed it." Poetic, huh? It means when you forgive, you bloom.

In short? Forgiveness is like cleaning out your closet. Get rid of that old grudge-jacket that doesn't fit anymore. Because you, my friend, got fresher styles to rock. Lighten that load and let love lead the way. Peace out!

How to Let Go?

Hey there, champ! Ever clung onto something like it's the last cookie in the jar? Sometimes, life's like, "Nah, let it be." But how do you drop the cookie? Let's break it down:

1. Breathe, Baby - Lao Tzu, the old Zen master, said, "By letting go, it all gets done." Deep, huh? Start with a deep breath. Inhale. Exhale. You've got this.
2. Ride the Wave - Socrates once said, "An unexamined life ain't worth living." Feel the feels, ride the emotional rollercoaster. But don't buy a lifetime ticket.
3. Space, Ace! - Remember Galileo? He said, "Nature is relentless and unchangeable." Give yourself space, physically and mentally. Nature will do its thing.
4. Chat & Chuck - Confucius was all about "True wisdom is to know the size of one's ignorance." Share your feelings; sometimes, just yakking it out helps shed the baggage.
5. Write & Ignite - Put pen to paper. Write down the junk. Our boy Shakespeare was like, "The pen is mightier..." Burn it or bin it. It's cathartic.
6. Focus on Now - Mr. Cool Hat, Gandhi, dropped, "The future depends on what you do today." Redirect your energy. Be here. Now's where the party's at.
7. Trust the Dust - Marcus Aurelius mused, "Time is a river, a violent current of events." Time heals. Trust it. Flow with it. You're not stuck in the mud.

Here's the deal: letting go ain't about giving up; it's about moving up. Imagine holding onto yesterday's pizza. It's good, but today's fresh slice? Divine. So, drop that crust and grab the new, 'cause you, buddy, are worth the freshest of life's toppings! Keep rocking and rolling!

• What is the purpose of suffering?

Hey there, superstar! Suffering? Ugh, right? It's like life's nasty hangnail. But what if there's a bigger picture? Let's dive deep:

1. Growin' & Glowin' - Buddha said, "Pain is certain; suffering is optional." Tough times shape us. They're like life's gym. No pain, no gain, buddy!
2. Life's GPS - Epic dude Epictetus remarked, "Difficulties show what men are." Think of suffering as a recalculating GPS. Wrong turn? It'll guide you back.
3. Compassion Compass - Our main man Jesus mentioned, "Blessed are those who mourn." Suffering breeds empathy. Feel the pain, and spread love. Cool trade, huh?
4. Reality Check - Confucius dropped, "Ignorance is the night of the mind." Suffering wakes us up and turns on the light. See clearer, be more real.
5. Soulful Storytelling - Rumi, that poetic genius, whispered, "The wound is the place where the light enters you." Every scar has a story. Tell yours, and inspire others.
6. Course Correction - Newton, the apple guy, said, "For every action, there's an opposite and equal reaction." Suffering? Maybe it's life's nudge for a new direction.
7. Bigger Picture Peep - MLK Jr. professed, "The arch of the moral universe is long, but it turns towards justice." Pain today? It could be a tiny pixel in life's vast, beautiful painting.

Alright, mate, here's the scoop: suffering might suck, but it's like that bitter herb that's actually good for ya. It's the spicy salsa that makes the dance of life so vibrant. So, next time you're in the thick of it, remember: you're just flexing those soul muscles. Keep groovin', hero!

How to find meaning in a world full of pain and suffering?

Finding Gold in a Gloomy World

Hey there, champ! Have you ever looked at the world and thought, "What's the deal with all this mess?" You're not alone. Let's unravel this, shall we?

1. Perspective Pivot - Good ol' Buddha once said, "All that we are arises with our thoughts." Change your lens. See the lesson in the mess. Positivity? It's a choice!
2. Connect & Reflect - Socrates, that wise bearded dude, told us, "An unexamined life ain't worth living." Dive deep into you. Discover your why. Make that pain purposeful.
3. Serve to Deserve - Jesus had a knack for turning the other cheek. Turn your pain into a mission. Help out, lift up, spread love. Boom! Instant purpose.
4. Starry Nights - Van Gogh (not a philosopher, but hey, cool artist!) painted stars brighter in the darkest nights. Dark times? They make the good glow brighter.
5. Ride the Wave - Lao Tzu says, "Life is a series of natural changes." Pain's like the ocean's tide. Can't stop it, but you can learn to surf!
6. Story Time! - Rumi mused, "Don't suffer. Anything you lose arrives round in another shape." Your pain? It's a chapter. Your story? A bestseller in progress.
7. Universe University - Einstein believed everything was a lesson. The universe got you enrolled in Tough Times 101? Study up, ace the test, and level up in life!

In the midst of chaos, pal, you've got the power to find the silver lining. Pain's a given, but suffering? That's a choice. So, strap on those boots, splash in those puddles, and dance in that rain! You got this, rockstar!

How to let go of the need for control?

Yo, brave soul! Have you ever felt those jittery "butterflies" in your belly? Yeah, we all have. But guess what? You're about to transform 'em into fire-breathing dragons! Let's do this.

1. **Begin Tiny** - Confucius nailed it: "It doesn't matter how slow you go, as long as you don't stop." Baby steps, buddy! Each little act adds up to mega courage.
2. **Dive into the Deep** - Good ol' Plato said, "It's easy to forgive a kid who is scared of the dark, but the real tragedy is when adults are also afraid of the light." Seek out unfamiliar waters. Get comfy with being uncomfortable!
3. **Squad Goals** - Aristotle, that ancient bestie, reminded us, "In the company of friends, we find courage." Surround yourself with peeps who lift you up!
4. **Epic Pep Talks** - Shakespeare wrote some killer lines. Whisper to yourself, "Screw your courage to the sticking place!" Daily pep talks = courage on tap.
5. **Fail and Sail** - Thomas Edison (light bulb dude!) said, "I didn't fail. I just found 2,000 ways that didn't work." Embrace fails. They're just detours to success town.
6. **Knowledge Power-Up** - Da Vinci believed knowledge vanquishes fear. Scared of something? Study it. Understand it. Conquer it. Simple.
7. **Celebrate, Mate!** - Every time you face a fear, even if it's just a wink at it, throw yourself a mini party. Positive reinforcement? It's the bomb!

Courage ain't about not feeling fear. It's about grabbing fear by the collar and saying, "You're riding shotgun, pal!" Keep flexing those courage muscles, champ. The world's got nothing on you!

Chapter 5: Spirituality, Religion, and Beliefs

Ever had your brain itch about the big questions? Dive into Chapter 5: Spirituality, Religion, and Beliefs. Who's God? How do we even connect? And what's up with science having beef with spirituality? From nailing your prayer game to distinguishing a Christian from a Pagan or an atheist, we're pulling apart the juicy stuff. No matter your belief (or non-belief), this chapter's gonna light that brain bulb. Curious yet? Let's roll.

Who is God?

Hey, ever found yourself staring at the ceiling late at night, wondering who or what's up there? You ain't alone, buddy. Let's unravel this big ol' mystery, tapping into the brains of some major legends from history. Buckle up!

1. Buddha-style: Seeking God? Look inside. Maybe God ain't some bearded dude in the sky, but that inner peace you feel when everything's just right.
2. JC's Take: Love, man. Pure love. It ain't about the church or a big book, but loving your neighbor as yourself. That's God for ya.
3. Muhammad's Word: God? One. Powerful. Everywhere. No pictures, please. Just faith and good vibes.
4. Aristotle's Brainwave: Ever think about the universe and go, "Whaaaat?" That first domino to fall, setting everything in motion? That's Him.
5. Lao Tzu's Two Cents: Imagine a river. Now, be that river. Flowing, powerful, eternal. That's the big G.
6. Einstein's Equation: You think God plays dice? Nah. There's a grand design, even if we're still figuring out the rules.
7. Rumi's Poetry Corner: Listen to your heart. Hear that beat? That rhythm, that love? Yep, that's Him.

Now, chew on this: Maybe God's not a concrete answer but a quest, a feeling, an understanding. Don't stress over the specifics. Focus on the journey. Keep searching, questioning, and loving. Let that divinity within guide you, and remember, you're part of this vast, mysterious tapestry. Dive in, friend.

How to connect with God?

Alright, let's break it down, real talk. You wanna get chummy with the Big Guy Upstairs? No VIP pass is needed. Just raw, genuine feels. So, grab a comfy seat, some nachos if you want, and let's get spiritual with these hot takes:

1. Buddha's Blueprint: Silence the mind chatter. Meditate, breathe deep, and find that stillness within. That's your hotline.
2. Jesus' Tip: Talk, man! Just...talk. Pray like you're chatting with your old buddy. No need for fancy words.
3. Muhammad's Guide: Rituals ain't just for show. Five daily prayers to set your intention and gratitude. Consistency is key.
4. Confucius says: Dive into sacred texts. Knowledge is power. The Bible, Quran, Torah – whatever floats your boat.
5. Gandhi's Wisdom: Be the change, pal. Connect through good deeds to serve others. It's like a spiritual Wi-Fi boost.
6. Mother Teresa's Heartfelt Advice: See God in others. That homeless guy? The cashier? Love and kindness that's your connector.
7. Dalai Lama's Two Cents: Nature. Yep, a walk in the woods, feeling the breeze. God's everywhere if you just look.

End of the day? No manual or app to download. God's connection? It's a vibe. A feeling. Dive deep, keep it real, and the connection will light up. Whether it's through prayer, service, or just being a good egg – you've got this. Stay golden!

What is the difference between religion and spirituality?

What's the Deal with Religion & Spirituality?

Diving into this topic, huh? Grab your floaties 'cause we're wading into deep waters. But don't sweat it; we're doing this together.

1. **Old School Plato**: Religion's got rules. It's structured and organized. Spirituality? It's freestyle, man. Your personal journey.
2. **Rumi's Rhyme**: Religion's like a map. Spirituality? It's the actual adventure. No reservations are needed.
3. **Gandhi's Gyan**: Religion ties you to rituals. Spirituality ties you to your soul. Different routes, same mountain top.
4. **Buddha's Two Cents**: Religion's external comes from teachings. Spirituality? It's an inside job.
5. **Lao Tzu's Lowdown**: Religions give you a path. Spirituality lets you blaze your own trail. Got a machete?
6. **Socrates Sips Tea**: Religions have holy books. Spirituality? It's written on your heart, dude. Listen close.
7. **Mother Teresa's Truth Bomb**: Both aim for the Big Upstairs Connection. Religion gives the address; spirituality's the heartfelt call.

Alright, here's the real talk: Whether you're a churchgoer, a mountain-top meditator, or just someone trying to find their groove in this wild world – it's all good. Whatever gets you closer to the Big Questions, go for it. No judgments here. You do you!

What is faith?

Got Faith? Let's Break It Down!

Ever tried catching rain with a net? Faith's kinda like that. It is elusive but oh-so-refreshing when you get it. Dive in with me!

1. Gandhi-Style: Faith ain't about seeing to believe. It's about believing when there's nada to see. Mind-blown, right?
2. Martin Luther King Jr. Speaks: It's like taking the first step even when you don't see the whole staircase. Yeah, deep.
3. Einstein's Brainwave: Faith's believing in the unseen, like knowing there's a tomorrow when we haven't seen it yet. It's trippy but true.
4. Rumi Whispers: Faith? It's the GPS of the soul. No bars? No problem.
5. Jesus' Jam: Faith's smaller than a mustard seed but can move mountains. Tiny but mighty!
6. Buddha's Insight: You know that inner light in the darkest moments? Yup, that's faith shining through.
7. Mother Teresa's Memo: Faith's the silent voice that says, "It's gonna be okay" amidst the chaos. Pure gold.

Now, here's the scoop: Whether you've got faith as sturdy as a rock or you're still on the lookout, it's all good. It's your journey, your rhythm. Just remember, faith's not about having all the answers. It's about being okay with the mystery. Keep rockin' it!

What is hope?

Hope: That Invisible Magic We All Need!

You know that warm fuzzy feeling when the chips are down? That's hope, my friend! Let's unwrap this gift together.

1. Einstein's Dose: Life's like riding a bike. Hope's the balance. Keep pedaling; don't stop.
2. Emily Dickinson's Poetic Touch: Hope? It's that little birdie in your soul singing non-stop. And it never asks for a cent.
3. MLK Jr. Drops Wisdom: Can't see the light at the end of the tunnel? Hope's your flashlight. Shine on!
4. Confucius Kicks In: When it's stormy, hope's the anchor. When it's sunny, it's the wind in your sails.
5. Gandhi-Styled: Hope ain't passive. It's the strength to swim against the current. Dive in!
6. Dalai Lama's Nudge: Lost in the dark clouds? Hope's that tiny patch of blue sky saying, "Hang tight, sunshine's coming!"
7. Nietzsche's Nitty-Gritty: Hope's the rainbow to life's storm, the silver lining to every cloud. Pure brilliance.

Closing thoughts? Whether it's a shimmering light or a roaring fire, hope keeps us going. It's that silent cheerleader whispering, "You got this!" in your ear. Remember, life throws curveballs, but with hope, you can hit a home run every time. Batter up!

Christian/Muslim/Hindu/Buddhist/Jew/Pagan/atheist/agnostic?

Unpacking the Wide World of Beliefs

Ever wondered what's going on in the spiritual mindscape of the dude next door or your friend across the globe? Dive in!

1. **Christian Vibes**: Ever heard JC's teachings? Love, redemption, eternal life? Christians are all in for that, following Jesus and the New Testament like life's playbook.
2. **Muslim Mojo**: Ever notice folks taking a sec to pray, facing Mecca? That's Islam. Rooted in the Quran, it's all about submission to Allah's will and the Five Pillars.
3. **Hindu Hustle**: Many gods, yet One. Life, karma, rebirth, and seeking Moksha. It's the ancient rhythm of India's soul dance.
4. **Buddhist Buzz**: Buddha's wisdom? Life's impermanent, filled with suffering. But follow the Eightfold Path and bam! Enlightenment!
5. **Jew Jive**: Torah's the golden ticket. A covenant with God, historical roots, festivals, and traditions. Family, faith, love.
6. **Pagan Pulse**: Nature's dance, ancient deities, Earth's rhythm. Pagans feel the cosmic connection, celebrating seasons and life's cycles.
7. **Atheist Angle**: God? Higher powers? Not buying it. Life's about the here and now; no divine playbook is needed.
8. **Agnostic Aha**: God's out there, maybe? Unsure. Agnostics hang in the spiritual "maybe zone," open to possibilities but not tied down.

Intrigued yet? Whatever the label, at the heart, it's about navigating life's maze, finding meaning, and connecting. So, next time, share a coffee or tea, swap stories, and remember: different paths, same journey. Cheers!

What is the relationship between science and spirituality?

Alright, grab a seat and some popcorn because of the age-old tango between science and spirituality. It's the kind of epic story that puts Hollywood blockbusters to shame.

1. **Buddha's Brainy Insight**: Did you know when you meditate, it's not just about feeling all zen? Science has shown it actually reshapes the structure of your brain. It's kind of like working out but for your mind. So, when Buddha talked about enlightenment, maybe he was also talking about some next-level brain gains.

2. **Galileo's Starry Wisdom**: Galileo, with his telescope, was like the OG stargazer. He believed that the universe was a book written in the language of mathematics. It's like looking up and realizing that both science and faith are just jamming out to the universe's playlist.

3. **Aristotle's Atomic Ideas**: The dude was onto something when he said nature does nothing in vain. Today's quantum physics echoes this. Everything's connected; every ripple, every butterfly's wing. It's all a big cosmic web; no spider is required.

4. **Jesus' Universal Love**: Ever thought about miracles? Whether they're acts of God or just science we don't yet understand, they teach the same thing: There's more to this world than meets the eye. It's a reminder to keep our hearts and minds open.

5. **Newton's Divine Gravity**: The apple didn't just introduce gravity to Newton. It was like nature's own way of dropping a beat. Nature's laws and God's laws? Maybe they're just two tracks on the same cosmic album.

6. **Rumi's Cosmic Poetry**: "What you seek is seeking you." Think about it. Our scientific quests and spiritual journeys might just

be two paths leading to the same truth. Kinda poetic, right?

7. **Einstein's Universal Dance**: Albert said, "The most beautiful thing we can experience is the mysterious." Whether you're marveling at a math equation or a sunset, it's all about embracing the wonder.

So next time you're staring up at those stars or down a microscope, remember Science and spirituality? They're not rivals. They're dance partners, moving to the rhythm of the universe. Dive deep, and who knows what you'll discover? The floor's yours.

Chapter 6: Spiritual Practices and Experiences

• What is meditation?

Ever had that itch to find the remote of your mind? Dive into the depths of "What is meditation?" with us, and let's unlock the wisdom of ages.

1. Buddha-style: Think of meditation as chillin' under a tree, going deep in your mind, finding enlightenment. It's not just sitting; it's awakening.
2. Jesus vibes: Ever heard "Be still and know that I am God"? It's about inner peace, connecting with the Divine. Just like Jesus prayed, you center your spirit.
3. Muhammad's take: It's like when you're deeply into prayer, feeling that spiritual connection, completely dialed in. A cleanse for the soul.
4. Socrates said (in a hip way): "Know thyself." Meditation? It's that tool helping you dig deep, get to know you, minus the distractions.
5. Lao Tzu's wisdom: Flow like water, be present, and embrace simplicity. Meditation is tapping into the Dao, the way of life.
6. Galileo spun it: Gazing at stars, understanding the universe. Meditation? It's peering into the vastness of your inner cosmos. Star-stuff, right?
7. Einstein, you genius: Imagine riding a light beam, freeing your mind from the constraints of time. Meditation's kinda like that, bending your reality.

Look, life's a crazy ride. Sometimes you just need to hit pause, find that inner vibe, and let the universe speak to you. So, got a sec? Sit down, breathe deep, and dive in. The universe's whispers? Pure gold.

What is karma?

You ever hear folks say, "What goes around, comes around"? That's kinda the street version of karma. Dive in, and let's break it down:

1. Buddha-style: "Man, what you do now? That's gonna decide what's up for you later." Like plantin' seeds; what you sow, you gonna reap.
2. Jesus-y vibes: "Treat others like you wanna be treated." It's that Golden Rule, right? You dish out good; good comes back.
3. Muhammad's take: "Your deeds? They're like a boomerang. Throw good, get good. Throw bad... well, you know the deal."
4. Socrates: "You think you're slick? Nah, man. Your soul knows the score. Be cool, or pay up."
5. Confucius's words: "Bro, your actions? They're like echoes. You shout good vibes; that's what you'll hear back."
6. Einstein, the brainiac: "Energy can't be destroyed, just changes form." Same with what you put out in the world. It's science, dude.
7. Rumi, deep as always: "Life's like a mirror. Smile at it, and it's gonna smile back."

Ever felt that vibe when someone's done you wrong, and you're like, "Karma will handle it"? That's the universe's way of keepin' things balanced. So, the moral of the story? Be the good you wanna see. It ain't just spiritual – it's life advice, plain and simple. Got it? Cool. Let's roll with it.

What is enlightenment?

Yo, enlightenment? It's like that "aha" moment on steroids, but way more profound. Let's rap about it:

1. **Buddha says:** "It's like wakin' up from a dream, man. You see the world, no BS, just as it is." No more sleepwalking through life!
2. **Jesus' vibe:** "It's like bein' born again, not of the flesh, but of the spirit." It's that pure, soul-deep clarity.
3. **Muhammad's two cents:** "You find the light in your heart, and suddenly, you're connected to the big picture." Divine GPS, you feel?
4. **Socrates' take:** "Know yourself, dude." It's like realizing you've been the MVP all along. But it's humble, not cocky.
5. **Lao Tzu spittin' wisdom:** "Let go, and flow." It's like cruisin' on a river without paddlin' against the current.
6. **Galileo, looking up:** "Seeing past the illusions, like looking through a telescope and seeing stars no one else can."
7. **Rumi's poetic spin:** "The door inside that swings open to more." It's all about inner vibes and connections.

So, enlightenment? It's not just some fancy, out-of-reach thing. It's about gettin' real with yourself and the universe. It's about droppin' the act and seein'. Think of it like cleaning your glasses after they've been all smudged up. Life just gets... clearer. Keep searchin', keep questin', and maybe, just maybe, you'll find your own flavor of enlightenment. Go get it!

What is the nature of consciousness?

Alright, hold onto your hat, 'cause we're diving deep! So, what's up with this thing called consciousness?

1. Buddha Might Say: Ever tried observing your thoughts? That inner chatter and those feels? That's consciousness. It's like the screen where all the movie of your life plays out.
2. Socrates' Take: "Know thyself!" That's what he said. Consciousness? It's the deep-down awareness of you being you. The real deal of self-knowing.
3. Einstein's Angle: Imagine everything's energy, right? So, consciousness? Maybe it's the energy that powers our thinking. The force behind the brain waves!
4. Lao Tzu's Wisdom: Think of consciousness like water. It takes the shape of its container - our minds. It flows, it adapts, and sometimes, it's calm and clear.
5. Descartes' Logic: "I think, therefore I am." So, if you're thinking, feeling, perceiving - you're conscious! It's that sense of existence.
6. Dalai Lama's Insight: Consciousness? It's like the sky. Sometimes cloudy with thoughts, emotions, and whatnot. But deep down? It's clear and boundless.
7. Freud's Deep Dive: There's what you know you're thinking, and then there's a whole lot under the iceberg. Consciousness? It's the tip. The rest? Well, that's another story!

There you go. Seven angles on that big mystery. One thing's clear: consciousness ain't just being awake. It's the grand theater of our inner world. Dive in, explore, and get to know your own show. Cool, right?

What are the different types of meditation?

Alright, so you wanna zen out and dive into meditation, huh? Cool beans. There's a bunch of ways to do it, each with its own flair. Let's break it down:

1. Mindfulness (Buddha-style): Stay present. Notice your breath, your thoughts, all without judgment, like watching cars pass by without chasing 'em.
2. Transcendental (Maharishi's jam): Repeat a mantra in your head. Over and over. It's like a song on repeat, helping your mind chill.
3. Guided (like a meditation DJ): Listen to someone guide you through. Picture a scene. Feel the vibes. It's like a mental movie.
4. Loving-kindness (from ol' Buddha again): Send out good vibes. Start with yourself, then your family, even that dude who cut you off in traffic. Love for all!
5. Body scan (Get in touch with your toes!): Focus on each part of your body, from toes to head. Feel the tingles, the warmth, the weight. A full-body hello!
6. Zen (Zazen, straight from Japan): Sit and observe. Sounds easy, right? It's deceptively deep.
7. Chakra (Spiritual energy centers, baby!): Focus on the energy centers in your body, feel 'em spin, light up. It's like tuning a spiritual guitar.

So, there ya go. A quick tour of the meditation world. Find one that feels right, and give it a whirl. Your brain might just thank you!

What are the different types of spiritual practices?

Alright, dive into the world of spiritual practices, and you'll find an array of ways folks connect with something more significant. Here's a down-to-earth rundown:

1. **Meditation (From Buddha and beyond)**: Sit or lie down, focus, and tune into your inner world. It's like giving your mind a spa day.
2. **Prayer (Used by Jesus, Muhammad, and many more)**: Talking to the Big Guy upstairs or whatever higher power you believe in—a direct line to the divine.
3. **Fasting (A hit with many, like Gandhi)**: Skip meals for a while. It isn't just about feeling hangry; it's a way to cleanse and get some clarity.
4. **Reading Sacred Texts (The Bible, Quran, you name it)**: Dive deep into spiritual wisdom. Think of it as the OG self-help section.
5. **Pilgrimage (From Mecca to Jerusalem)**: Travel to sacred spots. It's not just a vacay; it's a journey for the soul.
6. **Rituals & Ceremonies (Native American dances, Catholic Mass, and more)**: Specific acts, words, and items to connect and celebrate. Like a divine dance routine.
7. **Singing & Chanting (Gospel, Mantras, and Sufi Whirling)**: Use your voice to raise the vibes. Whether it's in church or a chant circle, let those vocal cords vibrate.
8. **Yoga (Lao Tzu and those flexible folks)**: Stretch and pose your way to spiritual clarity. It's not just for getting those abs; it's about aligning mind, body, and spirit.
9. **Nature Connection (Shoutout to Native traditions)**: Spend time in nature soak in the vibes. Trees, mountains,

rivers—they've got wisdom to share.

10. **Acts of Service (Mother Teresa style)**: Help others out. Whether feeding the hungry or just lending an ear, it's good for the soul.

Whichever path you vibe with, the point is to connect, reflect, and grow. So, pick your jam, and get your spirit on! And remember, the best practice is the one that feels right for you.

What are the different types of spiritual experiences?

Man, when we're talking spiritual experiences, it's like trying to describe all the flavors at an ice cream joint. Everyone's got their own taste, and no two scoops are exactly alike. But lemme break it down for you in a way that's easy to chew:

1. **Near-Death Experiences**: That 'light at the end of the tunnel' deal.
2. **Mystical Visions**: Like getting a sneak peek of the divine.
3. **Out-of-Body Moments**: When your spirit decides to take a quick vacation.
4. **Sudden Insights**: Mind-blowing epiphanies out of nowhere.
5. **Profound Dreams**: Not just flying or teeth falling out, but deep stuff.
6. **Miracles**: Unexplainable, wild events.
7. **Ecstatic Dances**: Body-moving, soul-freeing grooves.
8. **Sacred Silence**: That deafening quiet during deep meditation.
9. **Nature Epiphanies**: Those 'wow' moments in Mother Nature's crib.
10. **Divine Love Moments**: Feeling the universe give you a big, warm hug.
11. **Ancestral Connections**: Spiritual fam reunions.
12. **Channeling Spirits**: Cosmic walkie-talkies in action.
13. **Astral Projection**: Soul's out-of-body road trips.
14. **Sacred Geometry Encounters**: Universe's personal art gallery.
15. **Angel Sightings**: Random meet-ups with celestial peeps.
16. **Deja Vu Moments**: Cosmic reruns.
17. **Divine Intervention**: Bigger-than-you moments with a hint of fate.
18. **Kundalini Awakenings**: The universe's rollercoaster ride.

19. **Sacred Text Revelations**: When ancient words hit home.
20. **Past Life Recollections**: Flashbacks to your older, maybe cooler, selves.
21. **Empath Moments**: Spiritual antennas catching feels.
22. **Sacraments & Rituals**: Tapping into ancient vibes.
23. **Cosmic Love Waves**: Random love bombs from the universe.

Man, the spiritual world's kinda like a cosmic buffet. So many flavors to savor! Dive in, try some out, and see what vibes with you.

How can I develop my intuition?

Ever feel like your gut's trying to tell you something? Like there's a little' psychic inside? Let's unlock that sixth sense!

1. **Buddha-style Chill:** Meditation, buddy. Clears the mind noise. Makes space for gut vibes.
2. **Dream On:** Keep a dream journal. As Freud said, dreams are the royal road to the subconscious. Dive in!
3. **Newton's Advice:** Spend more time with nature. Those trees? Wise old folks. Listen up.
4. **Da Vinci's Doodles:** Start sketching or journaling. Get those brain juices flowing.
5. **Like Rumi said:** Embrace silence. Truth whispers; you gotta be quiet to hear.
6. **Aristotle's Two Cents:** Reflect daily. Self-awareness, my dude. Know thyself, trust thyself.
7. **Confucius Vibes:** Seek balance. Yin and yang. Calm mind, keen intuition.

Man, it's like tuning a radio to your soul's frequency. Keep practicing, and soon you'll be catching cosmic signals left, right, and center! Dive deep to find those inner truths. Ain't nothing cooler than being in sync with the universe. Peace out!

Chapter 7: Living a Purposeful Spiritual Life

Ever wake up and think, "What's it all for?" Or look in the mirror and go, "Who's that badass with a purpose?" If not, you're about to. Dive into the nitty-gritty of living large, spiritually speaking. From chucking good vibes around like confetti to rocking your final curtain call gracefully, we're deep-diving into the big questions.

Like, how do you be the good egg in a dozen? Or, how do you sprinkle a little love and kindness so that it sticks long after you've left the party? And have you ever thought about your spiritual squad goals? We got you.

Buckle up, champ. You're about to map out a legacy that's part love, part legend, all heart. Let's get this spiritual show on the road! Ain't nothing more epic than a soul living out loud. You in? Cool, let's roll!

How to be a good person?

Have you ever thought about life's cheat codes? Like, is there a secret sauce to being that chill neighbor everyone wants to borrow sugar from? Get ready, 'cause we're unlocking the legendary guide to being that good egg. And trust, it ain't all sunshine and rainbows.

1. From Buddha's Diary: Life ain't always a breeze, but yo, be kind. Just that. Simple, right? When in doubt, kindness out.
2. Jesus' Two Cents: Love your homies like you love jamming to your favorite track. It's all about that heart, dude.
3. Lao Tzu Vibes: Go with the flow. No, seriously. Like, don't force stuff. It's like trying to force that last piece of pizza down – ain't fun.
4. Good Ol' Shakespeare: Play your part. Every scene, every act. Life's a stage. And guess what? You're the star. No understudies here.
5. Aristotle's Playlist: Find that middle groove. Not too hot. Not too cold. Just right. Balance, baby.
6. Freud's Couch Talk: Understand yourself. Dive deep into that noggin. Sometimes we're our own riddles.
7. MLK Jr.'s Wisdom: Stand up, not just for yourself but for others too. When you see wrong, don't just scroll past. Be the change, mate.

Yo, by the end of this, you'll not only be the MVP of your story, but you'll leave a mark. A good one. Everyone's got that good in 'em. It's like the secret ingredient in grandma's pie. So, get out there, rock this gig called life, and remember – it's cool to be kind. Let's make it legendary, shall we?

How to make a difference in the world?

Alright, fam, you want to change the game? Be the hero in your comic book. Cool, let's cut through the noise and get real. Making a dent in this vast universe ain't a walk in the park, but if you have that fire, let's turn it up!

- Gandhi's Remix: Be the vibe you wanna catch in the world. If you're looking for peace, start with yourself. Drop that beat in your heart first.

- Mother Teresa's Blueprint: Small acts, big hearts. You don't gotta be a billionaire to shine. Just a smile, a hand, and a moment can light up someone's world.

- Einstein's Equation: Think differently. No, seriously. The world changes when you look at problems like puzzles, waiting for your genius touch.

- Nelson Mandela's Game Plan: Forgiveness, dude. Hold onto anger? That's like drinking poison and waiting for the other person to drop. Let. It. Go.

- Rumi's Rhyme: Spread love everywhere. It's like Wi-Fi, invisible, but connects everything. Dive deep, love deeper.

- Rousseau's Reality Check: Question things. Don't just gulp down everything served on your plate. Change begins with a question.

- Aristotle's Angle: Gather your squad. Teamwork makes the dream work. Find your tribe, and march on!

Look, making a splash doesn't mean you gotta be the loudest in the room. It's about ripples. You toss a stone, and it creates waves. So, let's toss kindness, ideas, and some old-school grit. Remember, every superhero started as someone's daydream. Let's turn those dreams into tomorrow's headlines. You in? Let's roll!

How to live a fulfilling life?

Yo, ever feel like there's gotta be more to this ride called life? Are you missing out on the main event while life passes you by? Well, strap in and grab the popcorn 'cause here's the reel deal on living life in full color.

1. Socrates' 411: "Know thyself." Get real with yourself. Dive deep into who you are, your dreams, fears, all of it. The journey starts within.
2. Da Vinci's Doodle: Stay curious. The world's full of wonders. Don't let life make you blind to 'em. Explore, ask, discover!
3. Buddha's Chill Pill: Be here, now. Do you ever try watching a movie and texting? Spoiler: You miss half the plot. Life's the same. Focus on the moment.
4. Plato's Playlist: Surround yourself with good vibes and peeps. They're like your backup dancers in the concert of life. Let them lift you up.
5. Mandela's Map: Find your purpose, your North Star. What makes your heart race? Chase it. That's your life's GPS.
6. Rumi's Recipe: Love hard. Yourself, others, that weird-looking dog. Love's the seasoning that makes life taste epic.
7. Hippocrates' Health Hack: Treat your body right. It's your ride. Fuel it well, and it'll take you places.

Life ain't a dress rehearsal. This is it! The main show. So, take the stage, rock the mic, and live your life like it's the headliner event. Every moment, every laugh, every tear - it's all part of the script. Remember, best movies have twists, so even if things get a bit wild, hang on. The climax is worth it! Let's roll those credits with no regrets. Lights, camera, action!

What is true happiness?

Hey, have you ever thought about what true happiness really is? Ain't just about big checks or dope kicks. Let's break it down, fam:

1. Buddha's Basics: True happiness? It's inner peace, man. You won't find it in the latest iPhone or that swanky ride. It's an inside job.
2. Aristotle's Angle: The dude said happiness is about living the "good life." It's not just about pleasure but purpose and doing what's right.
3. Rumi's Riddle: It's feeling that deep, soulful connection. Whether it's love, friendship, or that moment the pizza guy arrives.
4. Jesus' Jam: It's all about love, my dude. Loving others, loving yourself. That golden rule ain't just some bling.
5. Lao Tzu's Logic: Go with the flow. Life's like a river; you gotta float with it, not against it. When you do, you'll find your happy place.
6. Confucius' Clue: Know yourself and be true to it. Ain't about what's popping up on Instagram or TikTok. Real talk.
7. Gandhi's Gyan: Happiness is when what you think, say, and do are in harmony. That's the OG life hack.

So, here's the 411. True happiness? It ain't in the stuff; it's in the feels. It's about feeling right inside, connecting with others, and vibing with the universe. Life's short; find your joy and sprinkle that stuff everywhere! Keep that smile real. Keep it 100.

How to live a life of service?

Have you ever thought about ditching the "me, me, me" and stepping up for others? Here's the lowdown on living a life of service, inspired by some deep thinkers:

1. **Jesus' Wisdom**: It isn't just about you. Remember when he said, "Love thy neighbor as thyself"? That's some real talk. Help others, feel blessed.
2. **Gandhi's Gold**: "Be the change you want to see." Don't just tweet about it, be about it. Serve, volunteer, and make a mark.
3. **Dalai Lama's Dope Advice**: Kindness is the jam. The real win? Compassion. Make it a way of life.
4. **Mother Teresa's Teachings**: Small acts, big hearts. It doesn't gotta be grand; even a smile works. Give love, get love.
5. **Martin Luther King Jr.'s Message**: Stand up for what's right. Fight for justice. Let your voice be heard, and lift others.
6. **Buddha's Bit**: Give without expecting back. True service? It's selfless—no strings attached.
7. **Mandela's Motto**: Freedom for all. Help others break their chains. We rise by lifting others.

In the end, it's simple. A life of service? It's about giving more than you take. You are putting others first. And man, the feels you get from that? Unbeatable. Dive in, help out, and watch your life shine brighter. Be that light!

How to leave a legacy of love and kindness?

Alright, here's the scoop on leaving behind a legacy filled with love and kindness, inspired by some of the greatest minds:

1. Rumi's Rumble: Spread love. "Let yourself be silently drawn by the pull of what you truly love." Let passion and kindness be your guide.
2. Mother Teresa's Thought: Small acts, big ripples. "Not all of us can do great things. But we can do small things with great love." Remember, every act counts.
3. Mandela's Memo: Break barriers. Stand up against hate. Show folks that love is more robust. "No one is born hating another." Teach love.
4. MLK Jr.'s Jewel: Serve with a heart full of grace. Let compassion drive your actions. "Life's most persistent and urgent question is, 'What are you doing for others?'"
5. Gandhi's Gem: Lead by example. "You must be the change you want to see in the world." Live kindness, and others will follow.
6. Dalai Lama's Logic: Understand we're all connected. "Spread love and affection." When you get that, spreading love becomes second nature.
7. Confucius's Concept: Relationships matter. "Without feelings of respect, what distinguishes men from beasts?" Be kind to everyone.

Leaving behind a legacy? It's more than just being remembered. It's about touching lives, shaping futures, and planting seeds of kindness. Be that force of good in someone's story. Start today, and let your legacy be one that makes the world a little brighter and kinder. You got this!

How to die with peace and dignity?

Man, this is deep. Dying peacefully that's something we all want, right? Here goes:

1. Confucius' Reimagined Take: "We all have two lives, and the second begins when we realize we only have one." Understand and accept the impermanence of life. Recognizing life's fleeting nature can help you value every moment, making it easier to embrace its inevitable end with grace.
2. Buddha's Expanded Wisdom: "All things are impermanent. When you see this with insight, you tire of this suffering world." Come to terms with life's fleeting nature. By accepting the inevitability of death, you can focus on living fully and dying without regrets.
3. Epictetus Goes Modern: "Don't just wait for the right moment; create it." Settle unresolved matters. Tie up loose ends, mend broken relationships, express gratitude, or apologize where needed. Finding closure ensures you're not leaving behind a trail of regrets.
4. Dalai Lama's Real Talk: "Old friends pass away, new friends appear. It's just like the days. An old day passes, and a new day arrives." Build connections. Surround yourself with love and positive vibes. Be it family, friends, or caregivers, let the end come amidst warmth and genuine care.
5. Plato's Street-Style Wisdom: "The most serious punishment for rejecting to rule is to be ruled by somebody inferior to yourself." Make your wishes known. Be it through living wills, DNRs, or simple conversations, ensure your desires regarding your end-of-life care are apparent.
6. Marcus Aurelius Dishes Out: "Death smiles at us all; all we can do is smile back." Embrace life's natural cycle. It's not about

how long you live but the quality and impact of your years. Find purpose, let go when it's time, knowing you lived true to yourself.

7. Rumi's Wisdom Rewritten: "Don't grieve. Anything you lose comes around in another form." Cultivate spiritual or philosophical beliefs. Regardless of religion, many find solace in believing in a life beyond or a grander cosmic plan.

The grand finale isn't just the end. It's a reflection of the journey you've had. Facing it with dignity isn't just for you but leaves an unforgettable lesson for those you leave behind. Embrace every beat of your heart, every breath. When the final curtain call comes, take it like a boss—peace out.

How can I find my spiritual community?

Gotcha! Cranking up the wisdom and dialing in on that deep dive for finding your spiritual fam:

1. Gandhi's Deep Dive: Start with introspection. "In a gentle way, you can shake the world." Before you find your peeps, understand yourself. Reflect on what you truly believe and stand for. A strong foundation in self-awareness can lead to deeper connections with like-minded souls. When you're authentic, you naturally attract folks who resonate with your vibe.

2. Jesus's Expanded Wisdom: Embrace inclusivity. "For where two or three gather in my name, there am I with them." Don't confine yourself to strict boundaries. Spiritual communities often thrive on diverse perspectives. Attend various gatherings, be it a church, meditation group, or book club. By being open-hearted, you invite connections from unexpected places.

3. Buddha's Elaborated Thought: Actively Seek. "No one saves us but ourselves. No one can, and no one may. We ourselves must walk the path." To find your spiritual community, you've gotta put in the legwork. Join online forums, attend workshops, or sign up for retreats. By actively seeking, you increase your chances of finding folks who align with your journey.

4. Lao Tzu's Lengthened Lesson: Trust the process. "When I let go of what I am, I become what I might be." In your search, don't rush. Sometimes, the universe has its own timing. While you should be proactive, also understand that the best connections often happen spontaneously.

5. Rumi's Rich Reflection: Go beyond the surface. "The wound is the place where the light enters you." Open up about your experiences, doubts, and beliefs. The true connection lies in

vulnerability. When you share your soul, you find others who echo your sentiments.

6. Mother Teresa's Amplified Advice: Give selflessly. "Flare love everyplace you go. Allow no one ever come to you without leaving happier." Engage in acts of service. By joining volunteer groups or taking part in community service, you not only contribute to a cause but also find individuals who share your passion for giving.

7. MLK Jr.'s Enhanced Insight: Unity is strength. "We are not makers of history. We are made by history." Recognize the power of collective effort. Connect with those who share your desire for change. Attend rallies, workshops, or seminars. Shared goals foster deep connections.

In your quest for a spiritual community, patience is key. It's about more than just shared beliefs. It's about mutual respect, love, and a desire for growth. Keep an open heart, and soon enough, you'll be surrounded by souls who amplify your journey.

How can I serve others in a spiritual way?

Yo, wanna touch souls and make an impact? Serving spiritually is like being that quiet superhero. Let's dive in:

1. Gandhi's Vibe, Modernized: "Be the change you wanna see, dude." Lead by example. Your actions, filled with love and intention, inspire more than you can imagine. You don't gotta shout from the rooftops; let your deeds do the talking.

2. Jesus in Jeans: "Give and don't boast, man." Offer anonymous help. Sometimes, the biggest impacts are the ones nobody knows you did. Serve without seeking validation or praise. It's pure, and it hits differently.

3. Buddha's Fresh Take: "Your work is to find out your work and then surrender to it." Find your spiritual calling. Maybe it's healing, counseling, or just being there. Tune in, and you'll know your jam.

4. Rumi's 21st Century Whisper: "Let the beauty we love be what we do." Pour passion into it. When you love what you're doing, it shines, it radiates, and people feel that spiritual touch.

5. Dalai Lama, Down to Earth: "Happiness is when what you think, say, and do are in harmony." Be real, dude. People can spot a fraud from a mile away. When you serve, let it come from the depths of your soul.

6. Mother Teresa's Street Wisdom: "Spread love wherever you go. Let no one come to you without leaving happier." Small gestures have a big impact. A smile, a listening ear, or a comforting word – it doesn't have to be grand to be spiritual.

7. Lao Tzu, Real Talk: "Act without expectation." When you give and release attachment to outcomes, you've done your bit; now, let the universe do its thing.

And remember, serving spiritually ain't just about the big moves. It's in the every day, the mundane. It's in that smile to a stranger, that hand you lend, or that moment you truly listen. You've got a universe inside you, ready to shine. Let it out, touch lives. Make waves without even making a splash. Keep it real, and let your soul lead the way. Peace!

How can I leave a spiritual legacy?

Alright, hold onto your hat because you are leaving a spiritual legacy. It's some deep stuff, man. It ain't just about dropping a fat bank account for the next-gen. Nah, it's about dropping soul wisdom, love, and lessons that last lifetimes. Buckle up, here we go:

1. **Socrates in Sneakers**: "The secret of change is to focus all of your energy, not on fighting the old, but on building the new." Translation? Don't get hung up on what went wrong in the past. Focus on what you can create now. To leave a lasting spiritual legacy, concentrate on shaping a brighter, wiser future. Share stories, teach values, and set examples that'll help the next peeps in line avoid the same pitfalls and reach even greater heights. Remember, the life you live becomes the legacy you leave. Your actions, choices, and teachings? They're all breadcrumbs for the future folks to follow.

2. **Rumi Remix**: "Don't be satisfied with stories, how things have gone with others. Unfold your own myth." In other words, craft your own spiritual journey. It's great to get into from other folks, but don't get lost in someone else's narrative. To leave a unique, powerful spiritual legacy, create and share your personal spiritual experiences. This means documenting your journey, journaling your insights, capturing moments of growth, and then? Sharing them. Maybe it's through letters, maybe books, or just heart-to-hearts with the young'uns. It's about making sure your story and lessons ripple forward.

3. **Einstein Gets Ethereal**: "Only a life lived for others is a life worthwhile." Listen, the universe is vast, and in the grand scheme of things, our individual lives? Kinda like a blink. But what makes them resonate beyond that blink is the love, wisdom, and spirit we pour into others. To leave a spiritual

legacy, invest in the people around you. Mentor, guide, uplift, and love. Build deep connections. Spread knowledge, foster understanding, and champion compassion. When you invest your spirit in others, your legacy gets etched in countless hearts and souls.

4. **Mandela's Modern Message**: "What counts in life is not the mere fact that we have lived. It is what difference we have made to the lives of others." It's about impact, dude. How have you touched lives? Changed paths? Offered light in someone's dark moment? Focus on service, make a mark, and be the beacon. Engage in acts of kindness, build projects that give back, and find ways to connect and uplift communities. Your spiritual legacy will thrive in the spaces where love and service intersect.

5. **Confucius in a Coffee Shop**: "If you think in terms of a year, plant a seed; if in terms of ten years, plant trees; if in terms of 100 years, educate the people." Long-lasting legacies are about planting seeds that grow forests, not just gardens. To leave a spiritual legacy, think long-term. Foster spiritual education, initiate community dialogues, build platforms for spiritual growth, and empower the younger generation to carry the torch forward.

Ending on a real note, leaving a spiritual legacy ain't about fame or recognition. It's about resonance. It's about the lives you touch, the souls you kindle, and the love you spread. Live with purpose, pour out love, and know that every drop of spirit you share? It's shaping the world for generations to come. Stay true, and let your soul light the way.

Epilogue: Echoes of Infinity

Have you ever stared into the vast night sky, feeling the weight of countless stars gazing back at you? Each of those stars has a story. Each story is a heartbeat. And each heartbeat is a testament to the unyielding dance of the cosmos. This book is not just paper and ink. It's a symphony—a cry from the ages, seeking the essence of existence.

These aren't just words; they're soul imprints, silent screams from hearts long stilled but never quieted. They're love letters from existence, urging you to see, to feel—to immerse yourself in the depth of life's mysteries. Our time here, while breathtakingly short, is also unendingly profound.

Now, come close. Feel my heart, feel our hearts. This isn't the end. It's a beginning—a doorway into the infinity that weaves itself into every tear shed, every laughter shared, every dream dreamt. We're but stardust, you and I, yet within us lies the fire of a thousand galaxies.

Maybe there was a passage here that cracked the very foundations of your soul. Or perhaps a mere phrase rekindled a fire you thought lost. That's not by chance. It's the universe serenading you, offering its ancient heart, piece by piece.

Life is but a blink—an ephemeral whisper in the timeless wind. But in that blink lies the power to shake the heavens, to move the stars, to write tales that echo through eternity. Every touch, every sigh, every passion—it's the cosmos dancing, feeling, yearning through us.

So, as the curtain descends on this tome, remember: You are unique, talented, and awesome. You're a wild, untamed tale, a symphony of light and shadow. Each heartbeat, each tear, and each laughter adds a note to the grand ballad of existence. Dive deep, burn bright, and let your spirit soar. In the vast canvas of the cosmos, your soul is the brushstroke that defines, dazzles and defies. Embrace it, for the universe aches for your story. And oh, what a story it will be.

Also by Eliot Highfield

The Maverick's Guide
Massive Habits: The Bold Path to Transformative Change: Proven
Strategies to Achieve Your Goals

Standalone
F*ck Passion, Gain Expertise: The Path Less Traveled, The Rewards
Unimaginable
Serious Chat A Kickass Guide to Spiritual Life

About the Author

In the quiet spaces between the tangible and the unseen, I, Elliot Highfield, explore the resonance of the mystical. Raised in the bustling heart of Brooklyn, I learned early to seek the whispers of the extraordinary within the pulse of the mundane.My work delves into dream symbolism, the power of ritual, and the subtle energies that weave through our world. I am not a scholar of one tradition but a seeker who draws threads of insight from ancient wisdom and contemporary exploration.Words are tools for me to illuminate the shadows of perception. My writing blends personal experience, careful study, and a deep respect for the ineffable, inviting readers to join a journey of exploration rather than presenting myself as an authority.I offer my perspective as a fellow traveler on a lifelong path, seeking understanding amidst the vast, echoing mysteries of existence.